EASY VERSES FOR DIFFICULT TIMES

A life in six days of poems

DAVID ERDOS

PENNILESS PRESS PUBICATIONS
website: www.pennilesspress.co.uk

Published by Penniless Press Publications 2017

ISBN 978-1-326- 99667-3

cover image and all photos by David Erdos

For Aida Amidi

CONTENTS

PERSONAL TOWERS: AN INTRODUCTION

It was my friend, the writer and activist Jan Woolf who recommen-
ded me to Ahmed Mukhtar, a co-ordinator for the sixth Babylonian
International Festival of Arts and Culture. Thanks to her in March
2017, I travelled to a country I never in my wildest dreams thought I
would visit and experienced first hand the supposed birth place not
only of civilisation itself, but on a personal level a much sought for
sense of renewal. In the six days that I was there I experienced every
facet of what I was capable of as a creative person and gave reign to
every aspect of my personality, from the maudlin, to the inspiring,
from the naive to the philosophical.

Naturally when I returned home on the seventh day, I rested!

As the only British poet at the festival gathering of Iraqis, Iranians,
Syrians, Libyans and others from all over the Arab states, I received
tight pockets of acclaim from writers, audiences and translators. I
made a number of what I hope will be lasting friendships and met
and fell in love with the woman I felt I had been looking for for most
of my adult life. At one point I sat by the Euphrates and read what I
had written for her, to her and on the last day after an almost filmic
series of romantic moments strolled through the province at dawn. It
was a world and a life away from my suburban origins and reduced
the size of that world to the small enough span of my hand.

The poems in this collection (barring a few linking pieces, written as
I typed them up on returning to London), were all the fruit of two
moleskin notebooks in my travel bag. From my arrival at Gatwick
Airport, to my return to it, I wrote constantly, capturing what I felt
and observed as quickly and as artfully as I could, before reaching
the point that as I was writing one poem, I was making notes about
the writing of another. It verged on the ridiculous but it also seemed
important to capture if I could, such a life changing experience in
this way. A camera can contain what it views far more immediately,
of course, but can it be as comprehensive, or for that matter, discurs-
ive or, indeed, as impressionistic as a poem or piece of writing?

All I knew was that this was the only way I could function. The res-
ult of this may well be that each poem has a similar style or metre,
and if that is the case, I offer no resistance to criticism, and can only

hope that the potential reader finds some appeal in it. The point was to reflect a conversational tone to the observations, fused in a hopefully poetic manner. The search for the poetic facets of life – as opposed to just the poetry – is a constant in all of my work as a writer, actor, director and teacher, and so the title of this collection, alludes to style, content and indeed context as I moved between the storeys of my own Tower of Babel, talking to myself in the same language but with many contrasting tongues, while all the time working towards the kiss that would return me to life.

To walk the grounds of a place of such historical, political and spiritual importance was the truest privilege I could imagine. It is almost inconceivable to me that a dream of that sort found the flesh.

David Erdos, London, March 2017

PART I : TRAVELLING

Closer to Creation

BEFORE BABYLON

London is humid.

The slump,
                of late afternoon Gatwick,
Sweating its way into evening
After leaving my previous life in the day.

It is already night there,
While I am clinging onto these hours,
Before the unexpected trespasses
On the peripheral paths of the known.

I am waiting for a stranger to help
As I negotiate the first border
That separates freedom from
The tightened palaces of the known.

A clearly alternative world,
And one which exists without mirrors,
As I soothe each tense breath with reason
Before emulating
                the uncharted clouds of the flown.

OUR OWN WATERS

This moistening air
                    Is a kiss
Of either farewell or acceptance;

As if the departing heart
Crests blood's river
In ripples of doubt, risking waves.

The sweat of apprehension, perhaps,
Evident in the armed guard's machine gun,
Or the fear of the sandwich prices
Or the onset of my own middle age.

Kidnap, or crash, the sense of expectation,
Surprises. Am I a cause fit for dying,
Or a waste driven wound no-one saves?

THROUGH AN AIRPORT WINDOW

The sky looks mauve, alien, if only perhaps for this moment.
The falling purple unsettles, as if this were the last lash at colour
Before the slow rotting away, into night. My suit is grey-blue,
As I consider the passing fashion of faces; their disregard
Is as spectral as a soul you have prized, thrown to flight.

The ghost is peeled from the skin and is suddenly
Both arrival and departure. In the slipstream of thoughts,
My feared journey eases into a source of developing calm,
Slow delight. The journey is yet to begin, but look at the sky:
It is purple! Already the world is re-ordered

And the agenda reset for hindsight.

VISA VIRGO VERITAS

A problem at the check-in, as feared: to do with the visas.
All we have is a picture, a photograph of a pass.
A man, Mark, assents but then retracts confirmation,
Despite my name and those of my colleagues
Portraited and clear on the form. We wait an hour,
Then more. The Iraqi Consulate has rejected.
Meanwhile, our contact is locked within the hills
Of lost sound. We are orphans without home,
And without even a place to escape to;
Between states, we've been conquered and condemned
To remain the unfound. My passport remains at the desk.

My luggage squats before the conveyor.
We are Itinerants in an instant, Ignacio, Richard and I,
As we wait. The man in charge appears, frowning hard.
He will not look at me. No approval. Until we are legitimised,
We are phantoms, aimed to possibly haunt our own homes.
We are left in still air, as the planes around are cloud dancing,
The ugly girls at the disco, feeling no uplift or change
In our bones. Suddenly, our contact calls and the Official asks
For his number. He says this is him granting a favour,
But before he can do that he is graced. The conversation begins,
And he careens away, as expected, talking to Iraqi Consulate,

Baghdad contact and Allah perhaps, ear to face.
This negotiation accepts what we have to offer to the skies,
So it happens. We have just enough time to capture
The last security check and our fate.

SOFTENING

Flying together, Ignacio Lusardi Monteverde and I
And the formidable Richard Dumbrill,
Are unlikely brothers, possessed of an enviable compliment.
I am what I am. Ignacio is a maestro guitarist,
Classically trained, a Conductor and producer too.
Holy sounds. Dumbrill expands. Archeomusicologist,
Doctor, Lawyer. Expert on Unesco. Babylonian. Author.
More: Connoisseur. Raconteur. Pianist and restorer.
Consultant for the British Musuem.
Professor at Harvard and Yale. Anglo-French.
A Chef, a Gourmand. A profound collector of women.
We will later talk of Black Pudding
And the bloodings behind Babylon.

As we board the plane I am charmed
By these immaculate fellows. Flying high, I'm adjusting.
The plane slices the air like soft cheese.
I catch a glimpse, nothing more of an experience
I might treasure. From fears and foreboding,
There is the actual promise here of release.

DUMBRILL'S DISCOVERY: A CONVERSATION IN FLIGHT

Beneath where we sing, an ancient chord is still sounding;
The strings played by air moving
Between in the inveterate veterbrae of the earth.
Richard Dumbrill's Lyre, the oldest known instrument
Is located within his expertise and the hearing
Of some ancient God given song, through love's birth.
Only the layers of sand, the newly found realms,
The spent ruins can mute the long echo
Of the unravelling heart, and soul's search.

Slow contours of sound, shaping the land that now frame us,
The minarets as they mingle with the shadows of the towers
Struck down, can surprise and alarm before reminding us
Of the music that once coloured silence on those ivory sheets
Turned to brown. The Archeomusicologist turns,
Moving the mind's ear from Mozart,
Towards a new composition from the ancient day, fossilised.
Such discoveries now reveal the trials we are living,
Before the next judgement; subjects to an absence of fealty,
While calling for kings with coarse crowns.

After 4000 years, a student at Harvard or Yale,
Thanks to Dumbrill, re-imagines Babylon's beauty,
Through the concurrent noises of time.
A particular phrase, twists through the ghosts
Close around us; The unearthing of the Lyre
Brings truth's music, as all that was lost becomes now.

COMPRESSION

My pen bleeds in the heat.
Now compact black tears stain my notebook.
Alive in my hand, this foreboding of dangers to come,
                            masks the page.
It is a London pen headed towards a middle eastern expression,
Whose streets I will be running down to chase language
Before this dark distress forces age.

Set a word down, dab the pen to bandage the line of perception,
The notebook's face is scarred by explosions
Of the instruments instinct and doubt, even rage,
It becomes a thermometer, placed inside the mouth
Of the moment, seeking suck, it writes, dying,
With all of a terminal dog's last courage.

Any moment now, it will dry and from that death,
A fresh desert, on which can be written the will of the winds
Love has made. All of this from one pen
And its pre-Babylonian struggle,
Transmogrifying across silence
Before arriving at or on the next stage.

Air compression tortures the pen and so it bleeds
Through flight's struggle. Only the release of landing safely
Can relinquish whatever remains of its life.
Before the price can be paid to the laws of writing or death,
Or to the ear, as it listens. Or to the costs of hope,
Or to no-one; the full poet's wage.

ON WATCHING A FILM OF AHMED MUKHTAR AND IG-NACIO LUSARDI MONTEVERDE

As the two masters weave sound, flamenco and oud
Through sound's fabric, Ignacio's hands, primed by Ahmed's,
Inform each complimentary move of regard.

The men are connected by curves in the waiting air
Shaped between them; as one's eyes open to question,
The other's in affirmation, fall closed.

A short composition fanned, filmed for Iraq Television,
In which the interplay sets the template
For exchanges of speed and stilled art.

The slick entertainment and skill and the joy
These two men find in each other; as they perform,
They are music that shows the attentive heart how to grow.

IGNACIO WORKS THEN SLEEPS

Ignacio's life is pure sound, as Producer,
Recording Engineer and Musician.
I watch across the aisle, as on laptop,
He checks the treasures of music's sense through each ear.

The recording of a solo, ancient flute
Makes the surrounding air its cathedral.
Then, in praise, Monteverde sleeps soundly;
Through the waters of rest, music's tear.

A LIMERICH *(for Richard Dumbrill)*

As we get to know each other and talk,
And I read Dumbrill my poems,
He sets me the task of writing a dirty Babylonian rhyme.
A limerick's what he wants, and something no doubt,
Pornographic. So, I warm up with half clever
Before I try to subvert the sublime.

There was a girl from Babylon
Whose Sumerian wouldn't quite quit.
So to put him back in his place,
She uprooted tectonic plates
And let him fall back into ancient shit.

There was a girl from Babylon
Whose own were exceptionally fine.
To keep herself as a hit
She let anyone come on her tits,
Between 2pm, 6 and half 9!

IRAQI AIRLINE FOOD

Small new potatoes, spiced lamb, with miniature parsnip,
Slim carrot. Plum sauce, Prawn-rice cocktail,
A generous pack of butter, soft bread.
A chocolate square, cracker spread and a sunlight
Fused lemon cheesecake; beating BA, Iraqi Airway's
Pre-packed dinner could provoke a rousing appetite in the dead.

SUMMONING

In a war town land you'd expect
The barbaric present.
Yet in the sky's approach to it,
You see only the care eased from cold.

The tyranny of the heat as it builds
Is alchemised by detachment.
Flying still, I am cushioned
By what the divisions of cloud have foretold.

All will be well, if you can but believe it.
The days ahead proffer promise
Through which the remnants of fear

                      can be sold.

OBSERVATIONS

I

I am forever struck by the flimsiness of the aeroplane's window,
The plastic responds as if daring the outside air to assault.
Just as falling asleep on a plane is in the hospital league
Of endurance, what with the noise of the engines and time zones,
Along with the congress of the people locked within the bird,

Finding fault.

II

The sliding desks on this plane are almost as good as the dinner.
In their paths through air, the true winner
Is not the overly used, or prestigious,
But rather the suspect,
Yet guiltless and freed

                                    underdog.

AN IMAGINED INTRODUCTION TO MY FIRST PERFORMANCE

As-Salam aleikum.

From this phrase, I offer this:
My small greeting.

Beside the former palace of blood,
We are meeting

At the precise point of renewal,
And where the light sent to warm us,
Effectively channels gold.

A WORD SWORD

My pen wept. Now, it's aged. No longer primed, it takes chances.
Bleeding because of compression its last shot at luck is reduced.
But I will write on until death steals the line it shed across tissue
Or until words are halted in a terminal need to express.

Fighting on, it continues to sing.

TWO POEMS FOR THE MAN IN FRONT

I

The Iraqi head has a shape unlike any other.
Unless one means the Turkish head,
Or the French head,
Or indeed, the head in death, nodding on.
It expands in shape, like a bulb,
Doubtlessly seeking dark corners,
Withholding light. As I study, I see
That there is a difference in men to be won.

There are all shapes and sizes of course,
But the back of us reveals little,
Until you begin to appreciate that its contours
Make flesh a map faces mask.
I look at the man's hair and ears,
To see the face behind the flesh, the soul's visage.
The next step involves shadow and the secretion of self.

Breach that task.

II

'Turn off your light,' says the Bulb.
Please clearly being the province of English.
And so in the dark sleep's destroyer
Rifles his own with sharp words.
The displeasure of those who do not
And cannot entertain us:

Is this something to treasure,
Or the material to make swords?

A LAST FLASH OF CONCERN

David Erdos approaches Baghdad.
Nobody knows or cares about David Erdos.
Is David Erdos now fated to become
Another speck of dust in the road?

And yet we are not always our name
Or even the memory of it.
Sometimes we are just a poor correlation
Between what we choose to collect

and what's owed.

IGNACIO, RICHARD AND ME

Our conversation careens across careers and creation;
Connections corrected, as cavernous concerns coalesce.
A flicker of friendship, a flush,
Within the cheek and the chalkface,
As work awaits, fully catered we're crawling towards

Babylon's carapace.

OUR AIR FELLOWS

Creased passengers wake,
Having folded themselves despite seatbelts,
Hoping to be cleansed by this starlight
Purging the gutters of dream from each eye.

As I look around, Krakens stir,
Along with threat and potential,
Team Lazarus are returning
From their darkened private tombs and cave sky.

We have had snatches of sleep
With a full meal at night crammed within us,
The crew are now keen to fuse us
With the semblance of a fresh waking life.

But how will it end? Another place is approaching.
After six hours, you are as mindless as moths
Or fruit flies. All perception is gone
As you try to recover your body.
All you had was past. Now the future
Is simply a where. There's no why.

A LAST THOUGHT OF YOU

I have been thinking of you
And wanting you
In these heavens.

Below,
          Man's seeming paradise
Is the palace
For you, in reflection

To become the modern princess

Of sighs.

PREDESTINATION: A TOO EASY RHYME

From Hillingdon to Babylon,
The semantic separation
Is closer to the confluence
Of past and present revelation.

One never dreamt
That one could touch
The opposite of boredom.
Or anticipate and then surpass
The tales of decadence and whoredom.

A suburban boy at the cusp of time's flame.

THE DESCENT

Lights down on the plane as the audience sit expectant:
And yet there is no performance
Unless turbulence plays its part.

Fear, the understudy is quelled
And soon returns to past studies,
Hoping in time to be fearful,
Before Brother Courage arrives to take heart.

The plane creamed through cloud
And now a milk less land forms before us,
The body becomes thrilled with challenge
And the hopeful expectation of art.

PART II : JOURNEYING

Your Babylonian Palm

REVISAN

Half past six. We collect in an emptying lobby,
With a weariness that robs plenty of any sense of value or worth.
Visas are to be re-examined, explored as we attend their approval,
Chewing over dust in our clean way, keen to negotiate the absurd.

Distant guards, distancing as we coagulate before breakfast,
Three lumps of meat in the fry pan, with no heat on hand to be used.
Three itinerant souls, without home or nation,
A steadily softening trio suffering officialdom's take on abuse.

Baggage trolleys collide.
There is a sleeve of light through the doorway.
The absence of sleep stains my collar.
As another stranger coughs, some hope dies.

But it will be born again when an uncaring guard grants us paper,
On which to sign our allegiance to the Iraqi day.
And so, it seems, we'll survive. Ignacio has his guitar,
Richard his Doctor's bag full of wonders. I have my expectations

And a sense of building excitement, perhaps.
Will there be something here that has the power to change me?
In a foreign land the familiar is too often the clasp or lock
On the trap.

The light is staggering here. I look at it from this lobby.
God's manifest as a painting awaiting the sliver of shade I'd supply.

FROM HILLINGDON TO BABYLON

Paul, our driver attends;
A handsome Babylonian, like a hero.
Slick, popstar handsome,
But now, our baggage boy.

We slice into the heat of the sun.
Everything here looks so different.
Palm trees as resplendent
As their former provinces of employ.

The car radio plays, constantly,
The extended refrains of tradition.
The journey achieves transformation,
Translating my former feelings of dread,

Into joy?

OF THE YELLOW DAY

Of the colours here I can only speak in some variation...

Everything is yellow here, thanks to the ancient roots of the palace.
The air, trees are yellow, the colour of an ancient page
                                        that's unfurled.
The white of distance, sun-tinged. The ransacked air,
Curled or fraying,

Dust and heated leaves, chai, bananas;
When white grows old, yellow comes.

Even the blue of the sky, reveals the blonde
Of smeared oceans,
The yellow bugs, greened mosquitoes
And the withering stems of palm trees.

The searing glaze of the sun,
Infusing all with bright yellows,
The piss withheld, which falls golden,
                                        catching all of this on release.

The yellow is a thick envelope making us
The scorched letters in it, as we write about these locations
In which re-interpretations of life never cease.
You can breathe yellow here. The day in sleep,

Stoops to yellow. It is the tint and taint of the eastern
That makes the western gaze incomplete.

ON THE BEGGING ROAD FROM BAGHDAD

A begging girl stands with her Hijabbed Mother.
Stabbed by the heat, they move slowly
A toll gate of two, to the car.

The child attaches herself like a fly.
The window slides, like a revealing eyelid
Or curtain. The girl receives offered dinars,

As if desperation like this, were a tax.
There is no thanks, just the bank
Of the long withdrawn victim.

As we drive on, these ghost women
Are while being in debt to the heat,

Still attacked.

MEETING AHMED MUKHTAR

Ahmed Mukhtar, our host under the aegis of the poet, Dr Ali
Offers bread, eggs and honey, soft cheeses and dates at his home.

Muse and Master of the Oud, his humour informs every statement,
The Dry Iraqi transports us across the deserts and dreams
                                   he has known.
He is as realistic and warm as the climate of his country.
A rock star of the sand dune, a traditionalist for the new.
He walks into the room as I write, defining cool in all weathers,
Soon there will be a sand-storm of music,
And through what he plays,

                            Tales of truth.

THE ROOM GREETS ME

The palace is part of a dream from which the Iraqis are stirring.
As we arrive at the grounds by late morning
It is like Oxford Street, or Brent Cross.
No shops as such, only stalls, saved by a growing congress
Of people; Slick boys, hijabbed women, glimpsed
By my hijacked eyes, newly freed.

Everywhere that you look, people file,
Filling in the absence of Saddam.
Our bungalows, framed by Palm Trees
Are part of the complex he owned.
But now it seems simple here,
As the former wound is re-peopled
And I place my bags in cool shadow
Inside a palatial room, to be healed.

The bed is impressive.
Chaise longue and the most ornate headboard.
The wardrobe is a sculpture dedicated to Arabic design.
I am a convoy of words, an English ambassador for the poem,
And this goldening day is the parchment
I would use to make my thoughts biblical.

The room greets me. I bow.
From my own bungalow to these quarters,
The whole of the self becomes part and package
Of the divisions within Babylon.

WALKING TO LUNCH

Palm trees stand hand in hand with the redeveloping landscape.
Watching it adjust, Saddam's folly,
Is ransacked by the onset of reason, forgiving winds
And by change. The palm trees that once peopled the past,
Now provide a crucial link to the present,
As the strident leaves finger futures,
By detecting them, on the breeze.

FIRST LUNCH

Lunch in a room off Babil, the first of the communal meals;
Golden rice bowls, sparked with singed chicken, slithers of lamb,
Vegetables. We eat without language beside a table stream of Iraqis,
Swimming into taste, drinking water,
Which comes in a compact plastic box.

The men are generous as we eat.
There is a distinct absence of women.
Tissues for hands arrive bidden, as if parachuted in from soft lands.
I imbibe, hungrily, keen to fall close to the culture. The ornate chairs
Cram around me with people I can't as yet understand.

At the place of its birth the sense of civilisation impresses,
Granted as it is by the civil, with more graciousness than in England
Or from any insincere English man. This is not food as event,
But as its own kind of language. Not something to be refined

Beyond all sensation, and overpriced, packaged, planned.
This, after all, is the sweetest of congress,
Making even those with words frozen,
In the warmth of the day their own clan.

TO THE FESTIVAL

The festival has begun and I am to appear this first evening.
My Babylonian poem on Friday before a longer set three days hence.
We drive from the HQ of Babil, to the Ishtar gate, past the palace
Towards the large amphitheatre, glazed by two thousand souls,
                                                    sun ablaze.

A miasma of scents, the clamour of souls as they rattle
Within their separate cups and crashed bodies,
As people aim themselves at the steps.
It is a vast gathering and one I had not quite expected. Gladiatorial,
But with the Babylonian Lion, safe in his place and stone kept.

The trumpets of voice all resound in the jasmine air
And collision of more than two thousand as they call
For the love behind every sainted word to be wept.
I have entered the realm of possibly biblical truth.
You can sense it. In the broadening early evening,

You glimpse the outlines of change and old Christs.
To walk where they believe Eden was,
And where the Sumerians would have gardened,
And to give your small word creation in the shadow of that
Is profound. The blood rises. One sees immaculate wives

From past stories, moving like ghosts
Through the modern as your shoes and theirs share the ground.
One hears the prized past, and sees it too,
Through things quantum, as if theory was real.
I'm enraptured. As Adam's rib rips, in that garden,

In the theatre tonight, there's the sound.

AT THE SIDE OF THE STAGE

Waiting to recite at the lip of the stage,
                                    my mouth halted;
A supposed poet, in stasis,
As all of Babylon pushes past.

They do not walk around, or avoid,
But simply collide as they choose to.
If they do not know you at all, they won't see you,
Looking only to their chosen path, or to God.

It is not rudeness, of course
But simply their highly singular vision,
In which a westerner is occluded.
On a sunlit afternoon, I am fog.

THE MOMENT BEFORE READING

I walk onto the stage, with my bag, and this appears in the papers,
The later cause of amusement among various ministers,
But I am clinging onto myself in a quite different climate,
While besides me stands Riaz, translator and host,
                                    handsome, charming,
Whose introduction soon finishes.

I pose at the podium, squat, like a miniature Mussolini,
With only love in my pockets and the grease of dignity on my hands.
I read to honour the place and use my actor's voice to declaim this.
Salam Alekeim is the greeting, and I say it loud, strong and clear.
The two thousand souls say it back and I cast a grin towards heaven,
And then say the poem I scribbled straight out
While sitting at home in my kitchen, mind at that time dreading

But with a heart still sincere.

TOWARDS BABYLON

Babylonians all,

Despite the shreds and shards
Of past kingdoms,
Now a state of grace crests above us
As the sought for dove edges cloud;

On the folding whiteness we write
All manner of plans for lost subjects
Seeking place, their kings guiding
From the secretive realm of the soul.

What do we believe or attempt
To see in light's passage
As the sky fashions castles
Built for paradise to crush doubt?

We watch as a former Babylon falls
But in a translated breath quickly rises;
A restorative dream-state
That those with waking Hearts must allow.

THE MOMENTS AFTER

A round of applause that soon completes the sun's circle,
As I leave the stage, vindicated, a number of men bow and smile.

I take my place in the seats and a young man walks over to know me.
As does another. Here poetry carries all.

A woman arrives, praising me for the poem.
She gifts me two roses, one startling white,

One near gold. We talk of England and art,
Before her niece and sister soon join us,

The niece, Nadia, dresses herself to seem modern,
Hating as she does, belief's hold.

She rejects the constraints that her religion enforces.
She is both brave and impassioned, firing beneath social cold.

Ignited with verse as I am, I write her three stanzas
And gift them. She is hated by her fellows because

Of her particular need for release.
We talk as heat dries and the evening ices,

And this poem leads to another
And to the hope that she in turn, will find peace.

TO A YOUNG STUDENT

After the reading, an Aunt, an Iraqi supervisory teacher
Presents me with roses by way of thanking me for my lines.
Her niece, Nadia, then comes across to talk to me,
At seventeen she is forthright about what she knows and feels
Demands light. She will not wear a hijab, and for this,
She is hated. The courage of this moves me greatly
And I write a small poem to her as we sit. Almost, pleasingly,
She then weeps, moved more by my support, than my language,
And the considering of the future and the environment she rejects.
She will need to get the highest of grades to escape the path
That's pre-written. In thrall to the west, she seeks congress
And a new definition of home to perfect. She does not know
Where this is, or what she will do with this knowledge,
And in that mystery, our connection: two solitudes, newly
Refreshed by low sun. The fortitude of the young
Is no longer held by tradition. In its place sits the searching
For a completely fresh way to become.

BY THE GATE OF ISHTAR

The podium reconstructs the Ishtar gate to the city
As the words spoken from it, recompose the citizen's coming fate.
Admittance is all, seen in the weave of history in the brickwork.
In these fresh calls to new seasons the ancient codes are maintained.

THE PERSIAN POETESS

After a sumptuous dinner, with new friends,
I first see her at the table.

She will inspire more poems that sister this narrative.

She captures my heart and I am already torn between thinking
Of what I must capture and how it is I could live.

She will be here in the space as I write these next poems,
An entirely separate story that like the river beyond, ebbs and flows.

She becomes my main thought as I try to find ways to know her.
I capture her in a picture, and for tonight at least, no-one knows.

AN ASPIRANT

Naive again for some, I am sure;
Yet all I have to do today is write poems.
The pleasure of this, the full freedom
From worry or want is profound.

Perhaps it comes from new love,
Or the tinctures of love
Beneath senses. But I have been remade
And re-gifted as those after the flood

Attained ground.

And so let me avow
That I will now do my utmost
To grant the full picture
And as each details arrives

Set it down.

And so, to the toilets:

DARKER RIVERS

They consider those in the West the unclean.
The accusation's source? Toilet paper.
Because they wash, they are Godly
Despite the state of the bathrooms and toilets
That horrifies straining eyes.

How you attend to your arse
Is the line between the divine and the earthly.

At home the touching of paper turns sacred.
But in this context, is my holding back, sanitised?

IGNACIO AND AHMED RELAX

Ahmed's iPhone has a son,
A Nokia wasp small apprentice,
From which he translates information
To assist in the scale of his art.

Ignacio wakes from snatched sleep,
Roused by the dexterity of his fingers
Drawn back into rehearsed wonder
And the passionate embrace of guitar.

DR ALI

The festival has been arranged by the seminal Dr Ali Ash-Shallah,
He commands it. I wrote him this poem later at around 4am.

It has happened before, at other momentous times, other nations,
When a poet becomes politician and leads his nation state
                                                    into rhyme.
The joining of hearts with his hands as his reputation precedes him,
His works now are the people he attempts to astutely command
                                                    or align.

Dr Ali Ash-Shallah has become a symbol of change for Iraqis.
In Babylon he is building new walls and scales of belief.
He is working it seems, for the retrieval of glories,
Restoring each absence left on the land by past thieves.

All turn to him. Everyone consults Dr Ali.
Sacrificing time with his children, his wife as well,
For the cause. The rebirth of Iraq, through Babylon
And from Baghdad; newly edenic gardens

From which to enjoy renewed life.

MOSQUITO AND MOSQUE

It infects the air
As you anticipate its charged journey.
The noise intensifies.
It approaches, frenzied attack

In its sound. As the frequency shifts
And the volume spears through the silence,
You dream only of fire,
Or volcanic bursts through the skin.

Your fear of fever, or worse
As you pray for alleviation through Allah.
Under Muslim skies, the air soldier
Has bitten through walls to be found.

I will see its mark on my thigh.
The red hill burns as I touch it.
In a malaria nightmare
There can be no end to scarred dreams.

REPRIEVE AT BREAKFAST: CHAI

The smoke and the chai and the calm
Of location;

The quote and the lyre
And the balm

Of strong breeze.

The where and the why
And the sweet rules of difference,

The alarm of religion
And secrets

From a torn history.

THE BOYS BY THE BANKS

Ignacio and I take a stroll..

All the young men dream of home; mine as it happens.
For them, there is the thrill that is London,
Every one of them would fall prey.

They dress in strange style, an exaggerated attempt
Towards fashion; sculpted hair, ornate trimmings,
Skin hungry jeans. Swathes of blue.

They are dressed for nightclubs
But dance by the Euphrates and the Tigris,
And they prowl like the kelb, wild dogs

Who would happily ravage the new.
How many will stay and forego their imagined take
On my city, growing short, like their fathers

And bound to their birthing trees by sap-glue?
And how many will stray, like those dogs,
To hunker down on bone-changes?

One sidles up, keen to win us
And yet there is a kind of sleaze to his style.
It is like being cruised by an adventurous

Homosexual, while he protests that its English
He wishes to speak, all the while.
We watch them as they walk, hand in hand,

And dance by the river bank, bees and experts,
They kiss and reach for each other as they buzz
Across shit and honey for other worlds to defile.

MANLY AFFECTION

Why are the woman kept back
While the men show such love for each other?
The prizing of stubble is more treasured it seems
Than peach flesh. In their religion, male love
Leads to swift execution, so as they repress
They spend freely the only pieces of human gold they have left.

SECURITY

The security here is intense.
Every move you make is passed, prodded.
As the Babylonian Lion governs,
His sand blasted pups man the gates.

As you pass through you must wave;
A kiss on the air to show kinship.
To travel alone would bring fire to the breeding ground of your fate.

PRouD TO KNOW HIM

Professor Dumbrill's expertise runs as high
                                    As his avuncular spirit;
Knowing all there is to know he is gracious,
Granting with a smile each request.
A man of previous wives, along with countless books
                                    And encounters,
He stretches back to Babylon's famed beginnings
While discoursing lessons on the actual truth of Saddam.

His voice is French fused through the most cultured
                                    Of English,
Resident within Chelsea, Emeritus of both Harvard
                                    And Yale.

The British Museum defers as he proffers connection.
A Gourmand, his smile widens at the promise
Of food and of friends. He assists children, protects
And is both Doctor and Lawyer, Ambassador and informer,
                                    Raconteur, Pianist.

He is re-cultivating the earth and the way we have experienced it,
                                    Through lost music,
He is the glaze cast on ruins and something of his own Babylon.

Everywhere that he goes there is a flock of homing birds
                                    And Officials;
"Mister Richard!"
"Here, Richard!"

The Archeomusicologist digs, plucks and strums,
                                    To play on.

Richard Dumbrill at Lunch

A FURTHER FOOTNOTE

Man copies God with each pale belief system,
And as he does dims and douses, as it waters free from its source.
People like Richard Dumbrill are here to archeologise and remind us
That creative truth is revealing and that we have simply grasped
The wrong thought. The lesson is not to forgive, but to forego
The sin altogether. If Babylon had not fallen, man's bright
Impression would perhaps still bear the dazzle
Of time in the Sumerian's magic court.

FISHING FOR JESUS

As the Sumerians returned to the sea,
The tide they caused tainted others.
Religious organisations continued
Much that was formed by that wave.

From Cuneiform to clear form,
To the unborn messiah,
To Christ as an emblem
Of the ways to believe or behave.

Christ became then, the fish
At the heart of the nation;
The loaves of bread as the body
Were also a semblance of land

And man's shore. But the fish remains key.
The Papal hat has a fin tail,
A catholic consort, from which
The eating of fish soothes sin's chore.

It all reaches back, nearly every one
Of these legends. But the time of Babylon's
Grand beginnings delivered all that we treasure
From the ancient states to the systems behind modern doors.

AN UNEASINESS

Saturday.

Something is happening to me.

This is the seventh poem written before today's breakfast.
Not having slept, I am wires, that may in turn, burn me out.
I am a mass of red bites and too much food features in me,
And yet my mind is still talking. In fact, in this quiet time,

My mind shouts.

I am alive suddenly, as I know in my heart,
I have seen her.

We will walk today
And while walking

I will fall in slow stations
From this insects room

To love's cloud.

INSECTS BY DAY

The Iraqi insects persist
In their need for the flesh of the western.
The eastern wind does not stop them,
Drawn as they are to my skin.

As one moves to speak, the fly-thief
Arrives to infiltrate even language,
Injecting its spark, re-translating
As a steady deterioration begins.

The flesh, compromised
By the vow of the vermin,
As substantial as rats, the mosquitoes
Aren't quitting. In the fight

With the night,

Man won't win.

A LAND OF POETS

At a time of war, poets come, and this is a place primed by poets.
In every passing suit sits a stanza, behind every smile, a slick verse.

Under this Arabian sun, as a Jew, I am unrhymed or could well be,
And yet I have been made to feel welcome and free of mother

Israel's warped curse. The efforts of Zion appal,
As I walk the holy lands we should treasure,

Usurping God for man's glory, or worse,
For his political shopping mall, is obscene.

Here the Arabian fires burn even if I cannot understand them,
As I listen and attend to the poets

Who strive through the dusts of transgression
To honour their embittered fight to stand clean.

Voices of humour, attack,of refuge too and of anger.
Odes to the living and searing, soulful calls to the dead.

In a place of death and wronged blood
In which the secrets of the west and east

Intermingle, there is in blue seasons
More than the faintest trace of dark red.

Poetry stuns and this is a land where its treasured.
Young people crave it, while back at home they don't care.

Not even women read it, and it is for them
That its written. As I think about this woman I have met

And this country, I realise in an instant
That in this seismic clash, I must dare.

I owe the location that much. Not that I am of course anybody.
I am not a famous poet. Nobody but a few know my name.

But does that matter? No. We are only ever a part of the present.
What we find in death is the imprint of another light, a spent flame.

RECITALS

I

In the Arab states, every poet is published.
Unlike the teeming struggle in England
To rise above the rising tide of the few.

Every man has a voice, and crucially, every woman,
As their voices soar and intone, in the babble,
Babylon's stones cast no cue.

Not all of its good. A Libyan Poetess' voice channels China.
Her sound soon grows ugly, despite the dignified search
For her truth. The Egyptian Roué scorns, with mischievous humour,

As we sit in the front row, I become indescribably English,
As I attempt to smile at her, bridging their gaze, social glue.
She passes the Roué her book. He exchanges it like a napkin,

We joke. His derision comes from his own expertise.
I watch as he marks published books, a smile in his skin
Which you'd treasure. Everything about him a Teacher

That you would in turn wish to please.

II

To be out now in this green
In which every leaf reveals the next poet,
While strewn on the ground, words and flowers
Cast in and around carob husks.

Is to see how after war, poets work
To resolve the wounds and re-colour,
Not only the air, but survival,
Restoring bricks broken

By granting dignity to the dust.

III

How poets read their work must define
Just how it is consumed by the public.

Like the parent bird feeding fragments of grub to its chicks.

When a poet mumbles, or slurs, it alerts the ear to diversion.
In that way, the actual poetry stumbles,
Falling to the place the dog licks.

The tragedy is that this place
While being the opposite end to creation

Often contains the starred relics
Of the hopeful heart's evidence.

IV

Ahmad Shahawy passes marks
On this parade of the published.
A discerning eye, despite humour
To which I offer a mirrored response.

He fingers Allah's prayer beads
As a way to balance frustration;
When they are stroked he shows interest,
When they are pressed, his contempt.

Libyan is the mark for one pole of endeavour,
Babylonian is the finest, as his eyes close in rest,
Munching beans. A humorous man, a profligate,
A true poet, who is in touch with the spirit

Of what the tested word truly means.

V

The Syrian Poetess coughs
And continues to smoke,
While still talking.

It is a monologue that is endless,
Containing no doubt many plays.

In the palace room, we attend,
As I write this poem
To the unrepentent air
She phlegms into,

Dreaming no doubt of sweet days.

She was beautiful once, I see that.
Unfortunately now,
She has coarsened.

Across the beleaguered night
That she rattles

A certain lack of regret leaves its stain.

A SMALL POEM FOR HAFEZ MOOSAVI

With perfect dignity, sir, you deliver your poem
To a crowd separated by barriers forged from the word.
I watch as your heart filters forth

On this stage cloaked by rainfall,
As the storm in your thoughts
And joy-stations move across rails, soothing pain.

You have achieved the full gain, as befits any poet,
The genius of transformation that allows
The aching heart, love's full reign.

You gave me English copies of yours
So I return these impressions.
Your gentleness and your kindness

As I intruded and passed through such states
Is something I will not forget,
As I hope to love you and Aida,

But if I cannot, then remember
Just how much I have treasured
The time we all spent close to grace.

ON BEING TRANSLATED
For Ammar Alshalah

You arrived slightly late, which produced a slight anxiety in me.
I had no information as to when I was to appear,
But then you came with such grace I felt affection for you
Grow within me, as you were so complimentary of the pieces
Given to you to translate. In the pictured heat, we talked words
As well as clear context. How my long piece for my Father,
                              would need fresh emphasis;
And now the shorter poems on death,
Particularly my encapsulation of menace
Was in no way romantic, or human at all, in that sense.

My explanations became a bridge of experience walked together.
I was graced by your efforts while standing detached
From my words. You said it took you much time
But that you had grown fascinated
And had been held too by three poems,
Whose intricate thoughts you had heard.

It was a thrill, I admit to have these reflections of mine
Find new mirrors, across the realms of each language
There is a glitter and gleam on each page.

As the sun inked us both into a developing image,
I sensed the ghosts of my parents, smiling at me.
I was saved. So, thank you, Ammar
For the efforts you have given.
I will never forget this small passage
And the opportunity that it gave.

Just two hours on I would declaim these words to five hundred.
Including she who I'd reach for
In this and any other lost, golden age.

RITUALS

I

Dive down with the hand,
To pluck the food tissue;
A fast, precise motion
Much like the pecking stab of a bird.

As a pigeon in a park skewers crumbs,
So the dinnered hand seeks avowal,

On this soft page is written
The marks of taste and sensation,
And pleasure too, without words.

II

The constant gifting of water is key
In how to understand the Iraqi.
They seek to provide while reminding
That a different heat brings fresh sense.

Small soft squares from the stream,
Mouthfuls to down in one passage,
Packets of desire that you gulp
To be grateful, ensuring that all kisses quench.

They arrive in boxes, hourly.
One greets them, like brothers.
They are all that is needed,
Making a love for life's currency.

III

Three hours ahead, the Arab understanding of time
Is quite different. Appointments for waiting
Are not an unexpected part of the day.

Everything you ask for gets done
Just not perhaps when you want it.
So you must adjust and remember

That this was the place time was made.
It was not the Mayans, or Greeks
Or the inventors of watches,

In this place, calculations
Completed pre-existed our own.
We know more about Babylon

Than the Rome of Nero.
Here everything has a record
And is naturally worth waiting for.

They discovered the square root of 2
Four thousand years ago. Now, imagine.
It wasn't until 1650 that the western world

Marked that score.
And so you learn how to be
In the land of beginnings

Which are constantly changing
While rearranging the starting ground
Of the free.

SNAPSHOTS FROM THE SOUK

I

As we enter the Souk,
I see a Kelb dog in its dying,
Consumed by TB, its eyes glaring
At the other madnesses of the day.

These wild dogs prowl the night
And smear the air with their howling,
At a twist of the breeze they'd attack you,
Exchanging embittered revenge for your flesh.

Existing without love
And any of the West's soft devotion,
These are animals without glory,
Hair frames of bone, fierce friends.

The heat devours this dog
As it seeks sanctuary in car shadow,
The shreds of black like strands falling
From the desolate beast, as it ends.

II

The ancient market revealed.
Rainbow coloured chickens.
Chicks in a box.
Packaged children in an almost paedophilic display.
Ancient pots. Tourist tat.
The press and the smell of the people.
Lambs, kebabed, sparking sizzle
Against the unremitting blaze of the day.

We see a supreme minaret,
Like some alien craft, as a beacon.
A protective guard comes towards us
As soon as we arrive at the place.
And so they all escort us,
As if Militarism were touching,
I find myself moved, despite rifles
Assaulting my shoulder bag.

III

The market ages and soon we are walking into the near medieval.
A shop-stall of spices, bright against the darkened stone
And browned wood. Shadows paper the place
As the sparks of weapon forgers forget us,

As we saunter past they are working for the common tourist
Or perhaps the uncommon good. We amble. We taste.
There is a sense of time travel. The street is uneven.
In the ancient heat, pools of damp.

This is a place to align with the spectral Gods of all Bibles,
Whose darkened hearts singed the pages of holy books
And the studies of those who lived before the oil lamp.

I buy her perfume.
Which comes in a kitsch kind of bottle.

And still we move, across ages,
Poets, and Princes,
Tourists. Small kings,

Strangers.

Tramps.

At the final concert...

EHAB ELMALACHI

The poet as sandstorm performs to over two thousand people,
Each heart and throat provide answer to his street-speak and word
flare; Sentiments from the heart as the fired soul achieves purpose,
As with other worlds could such verses shout down the clouds
Through night air? This is a poetry as the pulse
For a slowly recovering nation. This could never happen in England
As all of its standards are glazed by celebrity's shit
And an ignorant hold across country. Whereas here,
Versed expression and the housing of such, achieves fame.

I watch as the festival reaches pitch in a diamond night.
Crowns and music. Ahmed and Ignacio's concert
Along with the other masters of song. I have been transported
And shown that the world I had is dead-ended,

And that to live again is to realise
That everything I had thought before

                                        was proved wrong.

Ignacio Lusardi Monteverde and Ahmed Mukhtar

ASSIGNMENT ONE

On our final night, Richard Dumbrill asked me to contribute to the official summarising for the festival. In contrast and complement to the dirty limerick he had previously asked for, this was a greater honour. He asked for a poetic prose and so I hastily tapped this into my iPhone, as the final concert continued and my aching heart yearned for her...

A festival is many things. In the faces of joy and celebration the history and practise of the featured location can be seen in every move and expression.

Having been invited by acclaimed Oud master Ahmed Mukhtar under the aegis of the venerable Dr Ali Ash-Shallah, poet and politician of Babylon to participate in that sainted city's sixth festival for international culture and arts, I have been struck by both the beauty and importance of the location, the generosity and interest of its people, the food in terms of its bounty and quality and the sense of liberation and expectation etched In every line written and each of the faces and hands.

Under the same skies that gave birth to the roots of civilisation as we understand it a nation of poets burst forth. Over six days of readings, recitals and public performance the fruits of the book were shared and offered to the gods of creation. Everywhere you walked the city of the palace showed evidence of renewal. The affections of men and the mysteries of women combined with hopes for the future city. As Professor Richard Dumbrill states, ' Babylon should be the first city recognised by UNESCO and not the last.' It's current profile post Saddam is hidden from the rest of the world and yet the flower bursts through the darkest soil and its petals contain a host of Arabic and invited western artists from Ahmad Shahawy, Hafez Moosavi, Aida Amidi and Ignacio Lusardi Monteverde through to Dumbrill along with a plethora of Syrian and Iraqi seminarists.

It has been a festival of art and culture unlike any other. Under each husk of carob we can find another poem and truth dignifying the shadows. This year has been a defining one in the history of the festival and at a time of political uncertainty and even madness in the known world, this festival has provided a lesson from the unknown or unfairly judged one. Listen to the poets. Attend to the artists and experience the majesty of long forgotten instruments as they call from the depths of the past to make that rare thing; a truly progressive but classically infused future.

21 March 2017

The later poem, Story of a Last Night *details what then happened to me. The organiser of the sixth Babylon International Festival of Arts and Culture, Dr Ali Shah then asked me to write an official report of this, the fifth day of celebration. Once again, recommended by Richard Dumbrill, I was duly honoured once more and set about, writing into another email, and despite the betrayals of a fast failing wi-fi. After several textual losses, I made the deadline just as my battery went. Thankfully the words saved and my breaking heart remained solid. However, all the time, cracks were showing, divisions I hope to be sealed...*

ASSIGNMENT TWO: DAY OF ILLUMINATION

Tuesday 21st March 2017 marked the 5th day of the sixth Babylon festival of culture and arts. Organised as ever with supreme efficiency by Dr Ali Shah and his ensemble of cultural lieutenants the day capitalised on events of the preceding days by offering a diverse range of skills, experiences and cultural offerings to the greater good and prosperity of Babylon as Iraq's creative, educational and spiritual centre.

After the characteristic breakfast of salmon bread, soft cheeses, hard boiled eggs and hot, sweet chi we gathered expectantly in the palatial meeting room of Babil. As the exotic smoke weaved through the air like a range of scented colours the time for the first event approached. Professor Richard Dumbrill of The British Museum, the Sorbonne, Casablanca, Harvard and Yale and all points in between was to give a token speech and interview on the future role of Babylon in terms of its UNESCO placing. In the grounds of the gate of Ishtar Professor Dumbrill accompanied by his translator Ammar Alshallah enlightened a delighted crowd on the cultural, spiritual and educational importance of Babylon and that legacy and contribution has been forgotten or overlooked by the mainstream world.

Prime examples of this ranged from the creation of practically every means of production we use to mathematical discoveries not made in the west until 1650 ad. That the Babylonians developed these processes four thousand years ago makes them as valuable and mythical a society as the Sumerians and supposed residents of Atlantis. It was a scintillating lecture introducing all the basic points necessary to re-evaluate Babylon as both a location and birthplace of all knowledge.

Today the President of Iraq sent a letter to Dr Ali praising the festival for raising the country's profile in terms of its UNESCO placing and so Dumbrill's words could not have been more timely.

In the afternoon we gathered once more for a musical concert opened and closed by the wonderful group, Maqam Singer, a stunning ensemble of Quan, violin and percussion playing traditional pieces and featuring the singing of Hamid Asadi. The opening pieces were beautifully performed by Syrian singer Mohammed Al-ashi with a power and skill that roused the crowd to joy while chilling them with the poignancy of expression.

This set the stage for a recital by Oud master Ahmed Mukhtar and guitar maestro Ignacio Lusardi Monteverde accompanied on percussion by Satar Jedur. The intricate weavings between the three instruments wove a blanket of uplift across the oncoming night, warming heart and ear and unleashing the purest dance of expression within the frame of all of those listening. Guitar and Oud are music's ideal brothers of string and the joint fabrics and texture they create perfectly sisters the heart. To see so many masters of their respective musical forms in such quick succession keys into the spirit of this festival. It is the delivery of a feast of miracles.

For the assembled crowd this human symphony of giving and celebration was rapturously enhanced by a stunning recital from populist Poet Hero Ehab Elmalachi whose non traditional dialect based stylings exulted the audience to a higher level of excitement than any contemporary rock music event in the west. In a country of poets where the word carries the soul of the nation, to witness such joy and excitement at the delivery of poetry was a miracle in itself to my English eyes. As the night darkened, the location of the open air coliseum like theatre became the finest venue in any terrestrial direction.

The ceremony concluded with the awarding of Iraq's equivalent of the Nobel prize, the Assad Monbarak prize. Prize winners were Professor Dumbrill, feted actress and star Hannan Chaqi, Egyptian master of arts and literature Ahmad Shahawy and. It was a fitting end to a day of wonder and accomplishment. As the crowd filtered out of the palatial grounds having experienced the cultural offerings of these magical stars of human attainment I cast my gaze to the astral ones above us and was aware that Babylon and this festival marking it, was the place not just of culture's beginnings but of it's continuance also. It was my honour to take part as an English poet adding my words to aural sea of rapture that made Babylon a magical island on land. Salam Alekeim. And may all your own miracles protect you.

And so the last morning arrived...

Babylon at Dawn

BABYLON AT DAWN

This morning, the last,
 I have Babylon to myself for the dawn hour, only.

As I walk its path by the river,
The cold of the sunlit air is tree-fruit.

It grows in separate breaths
As I observe every detail;

The mirroring river, the palms
And their bows, their carobs.

These drape from the trees
Like the jewellery of a woman;

One, whose 'poetries' in her accent
Are as delicious to me as all food.

I will be leaving here soon,
To either cut my heart, or revive it,

Babylon, the place of beginnings
Fills this moment now, where I'm stood.

I have lived an entire life in six days;
Fear, regard, the romantic,

A sense of achievement, friendship I hope,
And respect. Acclaim too, has come,

Along with such a contrast of moments:
Poetry at the Palace. A shoeful of piss at the gate.

Now, Babylon stains my heart,
Like some form of attack, or a tremor.

It has changed me completely,
And I must be aware of that change.

I must put it down, like this cold,
Despite a seeming profusion of sunlight,

To remind the heat all that's coming,
Moments after I've gone.

I have felt more love in this place
Than in all of the years since my Mother

Last touched my hand in her dying,
And now I honour this, as I write.

Walking around with this pad,
A sleepless and partly self conscious

Poet, in a place of poets
While knowing in my heart,

This is life.

PART III : ARRIVING

THE HEART'S ANSWER

That the journey ended with the beginning of a love that I am cur-
rently praying will last across a vast distance, was more than I could
have ever wanted to expected. As hinted at in the previous section, a
second story began to emerge for me on the second day of my visit.
It was one I tried as hard as I could to cultivate and what stuns me
now, apart from the beauty and preciousness of this particular wo-
man is that it should happen to me now, after a good deal of person-
al disappointment over the years, and in this particular place. It
would seem that if your need is strong and your call, clear enough
and perhaps, in the right setting, the heart can answer.

For a handful of days
I lived a film with her.
The dream has continued
And I guide it now, into day.

These poems are for Aida and come with profound thanks to Jan
Woolf, Hafez Moosavi, Ignacio Lusardi Monteverde, Ammar Alsha-
lah, Ahmed Mukhtar, Ahmad Shahawy, Richard Dumbrill, Anthony
Ofoegbu, Christien Anholt, David Ross Elliott, Ean Ravenscroft,
Paula Rougvie and Simon and Cindy Cash.

Aida Amidi

ON FIRST SEEING YOU

A beautiful face from Iran, lighting both day and evening,
Here in the city where life was seen to begin,
I find voice.

Blessings to you and all of your earthly endeavours
Joining tears from the mountain,
As they flow towards paradise.

THE FEELING BEGINS

The chance of finding you here,
Even if I cannot know you,
Is contained in your smile and full beauty
Which thoroughly warms every room.

Watching you arrive, or depart
I fall for the mystery of you,
As well as the sweetness I'd savour
And wish for again, all too soon.

How the world separates
Just a small chance of closeness.
I call to you across nations
With intimations of care, needs to know.

I want to know you at once,
To know all of you in an instant;
You, who are sunlight,
While Iraqi winds harshly blow.

Where are you? Who shares?
If you already have someone else, I'd expect it.
How can you not, when such beauty
Is there in each move that you make?
I have hungered for you,
But yours is a delicacy made
By your choices. These calls for answer
Are ways for the soul to find face.

So that it may weep through these words
All in the need to be with you,
All in the hope that you find me
And that having found, attain grace.

I offer you love in the small form of hope.

ON THE REALISATION OF LOVE

You will have to forgive me,
I hope.
          But when you leave a room
I now miss you.
To feel such things in a moment
And to wish and hope
They will last
Is such a powerful thing.

I am sad that soon the world
Will reclaim you.

Exquisite Persian,
For you and your beauty

I would unearth a day-star.

PALACES

I am in the Palace room now,
Outside the door to your chamber.
Framing my wait, people gather
But to them, I am closed.

Only the door's opening
And your hopeful arrival
Can restore or return me
To what I would share with you,

Or part own. It is the time before lunch.
But the wait for you is delicious.
I can practically taste the pleasure
As beneath my skin, blood and bone

There is a small, private song
That I would, if you wanted, keep singing,
Across these days of desire,
As I house these dreams of you on lost thrones.

THE WALK

I would like to say to you in a look
All that I suddenly feel about you.

Though I am aware this sensation
May well seem strange to you.

But as I think of you now,
After only a matter of hours,

The heart and my imagination
Have pictured all that we might say,

Share and do. You have enchanted me so,
I will spend these days dreaming of you,

Never daring to not, as to leave you,
As our countries part is sharp truth.

It spears the soft day
That I would share with you, only.

As we walk beside the Euphrates
In a kind of dream, I see through

All that I was, and what I would give to you
In an instant. I would leave my house

And walk to you, sit outside your door
And grow thin. Later, they would find me

In dust, with still a thought of you
In that rubble; caught on the wind, a lost rumour

Waiting for another chance to begin.
We are walking now. In the pause

The light has cast, in my mind,
A proverbial river of kisses,

I would draw you down to the bottom
And then up again, to each star.

If I can touch nothing else,
Then let your touch, your sensation

Be how I see the world as we're walking.
May this small selection of steps lead us far.

THE SEPARATE KINGDOMS

We talked of parallel worlds. In one I imagine now,
I can hold you. Just as perhaps I imagine
You wanting that hold as I do.

And yet here in the grip of a Muslim kingdom
I cannot and am not permitted,
And so I scour space to find you.

Risking something greater than sense,
To counter what I feel and stand foolish,
I am presently lost among people

As a blind man who seeks a clear view.
Only the star's savouring
And decision to shine is my equal.

As I think and sit with you,
The ripening world powers through.
We are each of us born from that star,

But the sky you house, stems from elsewhere.
I am listening now for the kingdoms
That the light divides without clue.

Soon the mystery starts. But already my heart
Provides answer. Across each universe
Of decision, the truest thing I see will be you.

HAIKU FOR YOU

I would have lain down
In the hall
To be close
To the place
Where you slept

AFTER THE SECOND WALK

You were a little distant today. I know you hadn't slept.
Had to see you. We had made our appointment
Which I duly framed with Haiku.

You asked me to call and I did, torn between
Wanting your rest and some of you.
This walk held more silence but the closeness

Was I hope, introduced. A growing feeling of trust.
It was all I thought to establish.
We went on our separate trips and I worried

But I also tried to relax. Ignacio, Richard, Ahmed
And I found the souk, our solidarity fused by intrusion.
Negotiating the ancient streets I discovered

A perfume store and gift rack.
It was the start of the Iranian year.
The few precious drops were delivered.

We rushed back to lunch where I found you,
Reaching for me, tenderly. You liked the perfume, I think,
Saying it was the year's first gift given.

I was as close to you as I could be,
Without being alone, properly. I am measuring hours now.
You have become a viable means of expression

By which the heart provides answers
To all of the questions to come across life.
I may have no importance to you,

But a day like this, holds a lesson.
That honouring is the essence
That husbands any man a true wife.

If just for now and this passing time only.
You have been breath and beauty
And restored my former darknesses to new light.

Thank you.

MY OPERA

Everyone wanted you.
I watched them swarm all about you.
Bees, round love's honey,
Perhaps a woman revealed was the point.

I tried to stand apart, without rights,
Not having earned your trust or your spirit
And yet seeking investment in a life
That I would fuse, channel, join.

It isn't even your face,
Or the fullness of your breasts, hips and body.
It is your eyes, your deep beauty
That I am sure all can see.

The way that you look at them,
Choosing to appeal, or show interest.
Your friendliness and your talent.
As you walk around, people dream.

I am dreaming you now,
Even as I stand here beside you.
Later on, as I type this and as we go on,
To walk through these grounds.

Aida for me, yours is the name of the Opera.
As the song is loud I sing for you, developing
Well, from love's sound. You could choose anyone.
Perhaps you have already chosen.

And in another room, other cities
There is another man you draw close.
But for now and for me, and from what I know
Of myself, and forever, you and what's given

Will be the things I want most.

I would come to you now,
Changing everything for you.
The scope and scale fills the theatre
With an unrepentant heart's dark outcry.

You have become, all at once,
A cause for which I am fighting.
A life with you would grant lessons
And show me at least, how to die.

TRACES

After stroking your hair,
I have the scent of you on my fingers.
The remnants of your perfume
Convey the places where, if given choice,
I would live. So much reward from one touch,
Or what such a small touch can grant me;
For this trace of you, forsake presents,
There is nothing else one could give.

WHEN THE TIME COMES

Love comes in a blush and in a rush to the senses.
The mind and heart flower opens, filling the field
And stone rooms. I see a possible life to be had,
And in the crush of thoughts and my wanting
I picture your face in all faces, see the day you'd beget
In each bloom. I am in love. Its the fool who truly understands
The illusion. To him, its real. All the others, fall like tears
From soft wombs. There are simply, hours of you.
Taints on the air. Night suggestions. All at once,
The bright future holds promise before my own tomb.

I am reaching out through the world.
Khoshgel, can you hear me?
If you do not wish to hear, then forgive me,
But I can feel no earthly shame, dreaming you.

CHALLENGES

And then the afternoon came, with another recital.
I was to read in the evening and wasn't sure of the time.
I had put on my suit and tried my best to be perfect.
People who had heard my Babylonian poem greeted me
In friendship and acclaim. But all I could think of was you.
I stood and talked with Hafez Moosavi.
His grace and friendship soothed me as he assured me
You would come. Then my translator arrived
And while time was running out, we consulted.
He was seeking some explanations while at the time praising me,
As I saw you arrive I was describing how my father's death poem
Was actually an attempt to align the lost and the living
As if one were talking of love, hopefully.

I sat beside you for a moment, glad you were there,
Then moved off fairly quickly. The Babylonian toilets
Do not share their birthing ground's state of grace.
When I returned, all was cleared and I had lost my bag
For the moment. Containing my life I had lost it,
Perhaps in a subliminal attempt to remain.
And to share this kingdom with you
As you had said how you wanted to live here.
You revere ancient cities due to the poetry in your soul.

After a frantic rhyme of despair in which I lapped the grounds
For my bag, like flies buzzing, my comic take on relief
Induced laughter. And I adore seeing your smile. The day glows.
And then it was on, towards the evening performance.
The fool had already written his tribute to the only royalty

He accepts or would know.

ANOTHER FESTIVAL

At the performance tonight, after a time apart,
I look for you. All of the officials are gathered,
As the central aisle divides us.

You are sat with your friend and mentor, Hafez.
I look down the row for your profile. You pass the briefest smile.
In such moments lay something joined, close to us.

There are hundreds of people behind as the Iraqi poets are reading.
Night at the palace as a cathedral sky paints the black.
I have written a poem for you that remains untranslated.

As I honour my Dad in Arabic, I want what I say to you to be fact.
On that podium soon I will say these lines as you watch me.
As they come to get me I pass you and see the way

That you look at me. It thrills me.
That spark is all that I want from living. You look down
The line. I look to you. I'd make love to you here, unredeemed.

You are all that I want and I want to tell you now that I love you,
Despite your lack of English words and my accent
That you sometimes find hard to hear.

I will read my father's tribute loudly
And as you say later on, like an actor,
But all of it in preparation, in order to tell this part of the world,

What is clear. That you are the one that I have been looking for.
I am certain. I would give my life to you, breath by breath,
Year to year. Until I am dead, much like my beloved parents.

I share you now with them as another spectacular part of the night.
Here we are taking part at a Festival as two poets.

Tonight in my reading, I am both alive and a ghost.

If you do not love me, I'll live but the chance of you
Will be haunting. And so seizing life, I read to you,
In a festival others founded.

For now it is ours, all fear closed.

AIDA

I will let mosquitoes ruin my legs if it leads you to walk to me.
I will let storms cloud my answers and intemperate winds
                                        steal my face.
After falling, I'd wake to see you as reward for the chasm;
In time, across journeys, you will be my destination in age.

I will write to you, every day until you learn how to love me.
In all I write, you're the shadow waiting behind the next page.
In a handful of breath you have given me something to cherish.
You. This desire has re-ordered the heart for love's space.

MOURNING OF THE DAY BEFORE WE LEAVE

I long to see Hafez Moosavi's cap in approach
Because then I know you'll be coming,
Cresting the leaves across distance
That is soon to be echoed through time.

Too soon, you will pass, as the birds,
Sectioned by the part of the sky you live under,
And I will strain the clouds above England,
Each in an attempt to see through.

How will the flight of this unwanted change
Now affect me? How does the cloud feel when subtracted
From its chosen place beside light?
In two days you'll become a necessary part

Of my landscape. My world forms around you;
The world that I try to make as I write.
It is the last morning. Today will take the best of you.
I will crave and carve from the evening

Any heated ember I can find in moonlight.
And there are not many, I'm sure.
I will wait the day out to see you.
You have promised six o clock, maybe seven.
Ten hours to go. Love is plight.

WHAT YOU GIVE

You call your work, 'poetries'
And I love the way that you say it.
The sound of your speech is air moving
In and out of the cloud.

Then there is your softness of you;
Voice, smile. Then your body.
Your remarkable eyes looking through me,
Absolving away any doubt.

After only a day I loved you,
A feeling graced from one moment.
Your Poetries frame a kingdom
In which any ragged listener can be crowned.

STORY OF A LAST NIGHT

When you didn't arrive I was lost. The day turned to fire.
Burning paranoia, need, worry, all under the most perfect of skies.
And yet I worked hard for calm, accompanying Richard's lecture.
Before rushing back to keep waiting despite the remaining hours
To pass. We were called to the festival around four. I had to go,
Duly hoping that you would appear as dear Riaz was I thought
The night's host. Another man took his place and the performance
Seemed endless. It was riven with beauty while it was only yours
That I sought. I think I behaved shamefully and forced myself back
To decorum. Richard won his prize and assured me that I would
Win one as a contributor too. But you were not there, so clearly
That wouldn't happen. Appearing as well, recognition would have
Been for everyone, I was sure. I jumped in a car, desperate because
Of the hours. We would be leaving on Wednesday and here we were,
Half past nine, Tuesday night.

I sat in the hall, despite the graceful ebony of the evening.
Babylon in mooned darkness is as beautiful as it's pure.
The wi-fi went on and off and the artistic wife I so wanted,
Was still in Baghdad. I was worried.
Had something happened to you all? I was scared.
But then I was asked to write and I wrote on a mobile phone
My impressions, losing three versions to signal and feeling terrible
Waves of unease. You said you had changed your room
To be close so I kept checking to see if you had returned.
I kept writing. Then Ahmed told me that because it was
Iranian New Year you probably wouldn't return.
I could feel my heart break, two visible halves. Toffee shatters.
As I felt the sweetness with which you had filled me fall
Across stone.

It was an emotional wave that certainly drowned this small swimmer.
I had prayed not to miss you. And here I was now, alone.
I frittered the minutes, focused and finished typing.
As the final words left my fingers, my battery died. I near screamed.
I ran back for my charger, legs weak, then scrambled my words
Back to effort. Seeking help, it was emailed, yet I was

Left incomplete. I had the neglected sadness of dogs,
Awaiting their absent master or mistress.
On the palace steps I looked for you, despite knowing then
You'd not come.

I could only write a letter and hope that at some point
You would find it. My accent is difficult for you,
So now the written word had a function, containing everything
I'd become. As I started it in the hall you walked through the door.
You were smiling. You had been celebrating and looked to me
Like night sun. I have had distress in my life
But the joy of seeing you was a bandage.
Talking to you returned senses I thought and feared I had lost.
I unburdened my heart. I'm sorry if this clouded your evening.
I had to say things in case this was the only time we would meet.
You held my hand as I told you I would change my life for you.
And I would. I promise. I would do everything.
We returned to our rooms. You were cold.
And so I gave you my blanket. I wouldn't sleep,
But around you, the knowledge of that would present me
With the love, warmth and comfort of anything else I would need.

AT THREE IN THE MORNING

Kissing you is the cup
From which the weary traveller takes renewal.

Holding you is belonging to the scented house on the hill.

Touching your face, or your back, your arm, your hair
Is such music.

Looking at you looking at me
Teaches eyes, then soul what to feel.

I love you. Its plain.
Even if you do not love me.
That barely matters,
Not in the other unbalances found in life.

All we need is to feel.
All we hope for now is a moment.
In which a man who was lonely
Has for some minutes
Kissed the only woman
He could ever want as his wife.

LEAVING

Early morning. I walk.

The river machine is still working.
A tiny boat swans the mirror of its perfect face.
That face, yours. There is simply the river and you,
The climate of the air and these senses
That have kept me from my sleep,
My day dreaming will now always be of your truth.

I sit in the place where we sat
And realise that love is a mirror, reflecting back
Our desires and what these days on earth can be for.

You are as much a part of my heart
As the blood moving through it,
As I am this morning, moving around Babylon
After Dawn. Now this place is my heart,
And you are the soft reason for it.
You slept in my blanket and the joy of that
Brings release. I will fight to know you,
So that all I knew before apes the river,
Reflecting back, like a mirror,
Something on the other shore, lost but free.

Where will this end?
Ah, well, you see for that, there's no language.
Only the heart knows and answers
And as the tales told have shown us,
There is no reprieve.

No heart speaks.

CODA: HALF HAIKU FOR YOU

Chosen girl
Of

     my dreams,

You're

The day.

On joining a past and future love...

ANOTHER MOTHER
Mother's Day 2017,

For Cindy, Marc, Karen, Bob, Jeff, Matt, David, Katie, David Ross,
Sara, Sarah B, and all of my siblings in loss

When the unthinkable strikes,
The head and the heart are both emptied,
Just as, perhaps, for a mother, once the child is born,
The void's moist. After her death, this small space
Grows irredeemably larger. And so on this day,
Of mothers, I must mourn for my own. I've no choice.

I would like her to enter the room
And consider the changes within it.
I sense her fast disapproval, while also hoping
That she still understands, that the clatter of books
Is a kind of company for me, after five years separation
And the sadness of where we both are, all's unplanned.

But to all of my friends who still retain
Their own mothers, I offer my celebration and urge you
To seek as much time with them as you can.
For when the space opens up and you have only one English day
To remind you, you will recognise that each moment
Calls for the child to cry madly before the lost sanity of her hands.